Picture credits:
National Oceanic and Atmospheric Administration (NOAA): 35 top left,
12 top right; Dave Gatley/FEMA News: 41 bottom

Copyright: Really Useful Map Company (HK) Ltd.
Published By: Robert Frederick Ltd.
4 North Parade Bath, England.
First Published: 2005
Printed in India

All rights reserved. No part of this publication may be reported,
stored in a retrieval system or transmitted, in any form or by any means,
electronic, mechanical, photocopying, recording, or otherwise, without
the prior permission of the copyright holder.

WILD WEATHER

CONTENTS

What's the Weather Like?	6
Sun and Water	8
Wind and Cloud	10
Seasons	12
Climates	14
Humid and Hot	16
Storming the Skies	18
Thunder and Lightning	20
Weather Wash	22
As Cold as Can Be	24
Snow, Hail and Ice	26
When Storms Strike	28
Drought Disasters	30
Weather Watch	32
Eye in the Sky	34
Changing Weather	36
Weather Woes	38
Weather or What!	40
Fascinating Facts	42
Glossary	44

What's the Weather Like?

When you look out of the house to see if it's a sunny, windy or rainy day, you are checking the weather. Weather is the state of the atmosphere or the air that surrounds the Earth at a particular time. It may be hot or cold, cloudy or clear, windy or calm.

Climatic factor

Weather is not the same as climate. While weather is the condition of air over a short period – a few hours to a few days, climate is the average weather condition over a long time, usually 10-30 years.

Life matters

Weather affects farming practises. Farmers need clear weather to plant and harvest their crops. Plants need sunlight and rainfall to grow, but a storm or sudden frost can damage crops.

▼ *Plantation of crops is dependent on weather conditions. In some countries, crops are planted only when rains are expected*

◀ *We wear woollen clothing in winter to trap heat close to our body*

INTERESTING FACT

People who study the weather are called meteorologists. They can also predict weather. Such forecasts are aired on television and published in newspapers.

FACT FILE

- **Highest temperature:** 58°C, in El Azizia, Libya
- **Lowest temperature:** -89°C, in Vostok, Antarctica
- **Highest rainfall in a year:** 2,647 cm, in Cherrapunji, India
- **Lowest average annual rainfall:** 0.03 inches (about 0.8 mm), in Arica, Chile

Grey or chirpy

Changing weather affects our lives in many ways. We dress according to the weather, choosing heavy woollens when cold and dressing lightly if it is hot. Weather can even have an effect on one's mood!

Killer weather

Industries, transportation and communication also suffer in bad weather. Severe weather conditions like tornadoes, storms and blizzards can even kill people. When weather turns wild, it is often impossible to find cover!

▶ *Weather can change every few hours in a day. A bright sunny morning can turn gloomy and rainy by noon*

Sun and Water

The conditions that influence the weather include wind, pressure, temperature, humidity, clouds and precipitation. Nearly all weather changes occur in the lowest layer of the atmosphere, called the troposphere.

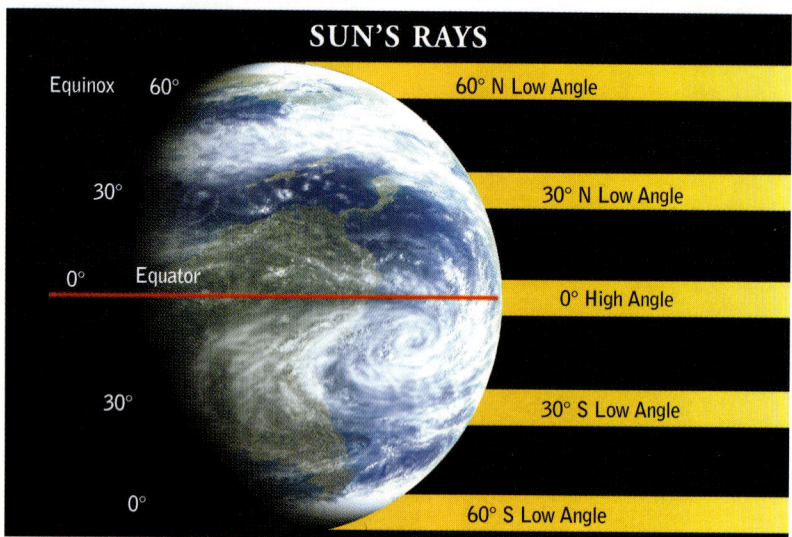

▲ The Sun's rays fall directly on the Equator, making it the hottest area. The North Pole and the South Pole are the coldest, since the Sun's rays strike them at an angle

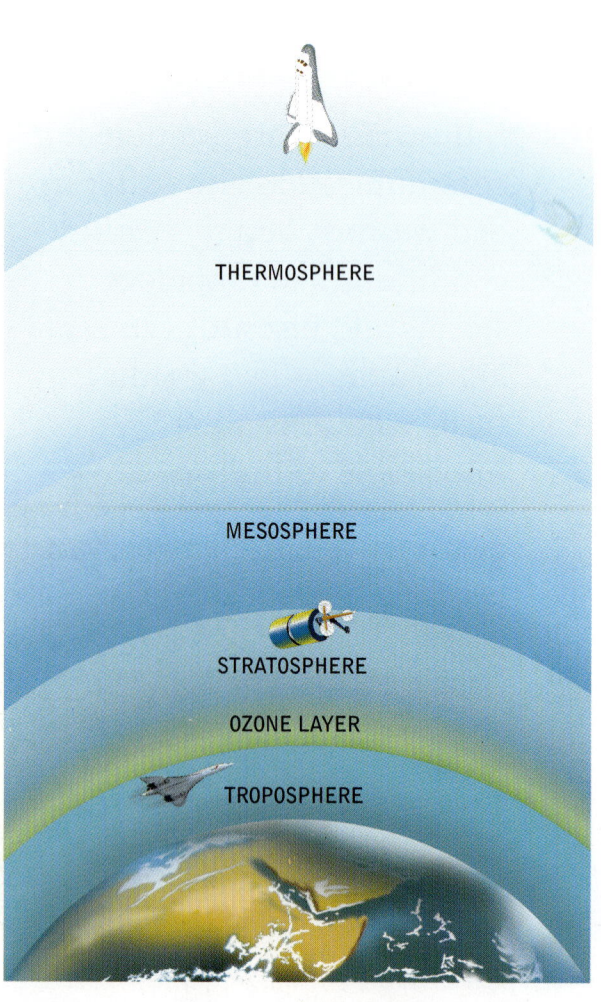

Starting with the Sun

The Sun's energy heats certain parts of the Earth more than others. The unequal heating leads to variations in temperature, wind, air pressure and ocean currents. This causes weather changes.

Temperature changes

Hot air is lighter than cold air. As air gets heated, it rises up and cold air gushes in to take its place. This causes wind, which can be as slow as a gentle breeze, or fast and raging like a fierce storm.

◄ Apart from weather changes, the atmosphere also protects us from the Sun's harmful radiation

Evaporating water

The Sun also causes the water cycle – the process by which water circulates between land and air, forming clouds and rain. The Sun heats up water in rivers, lakes and oceans, and turns it into vapour. This is called evaporation.

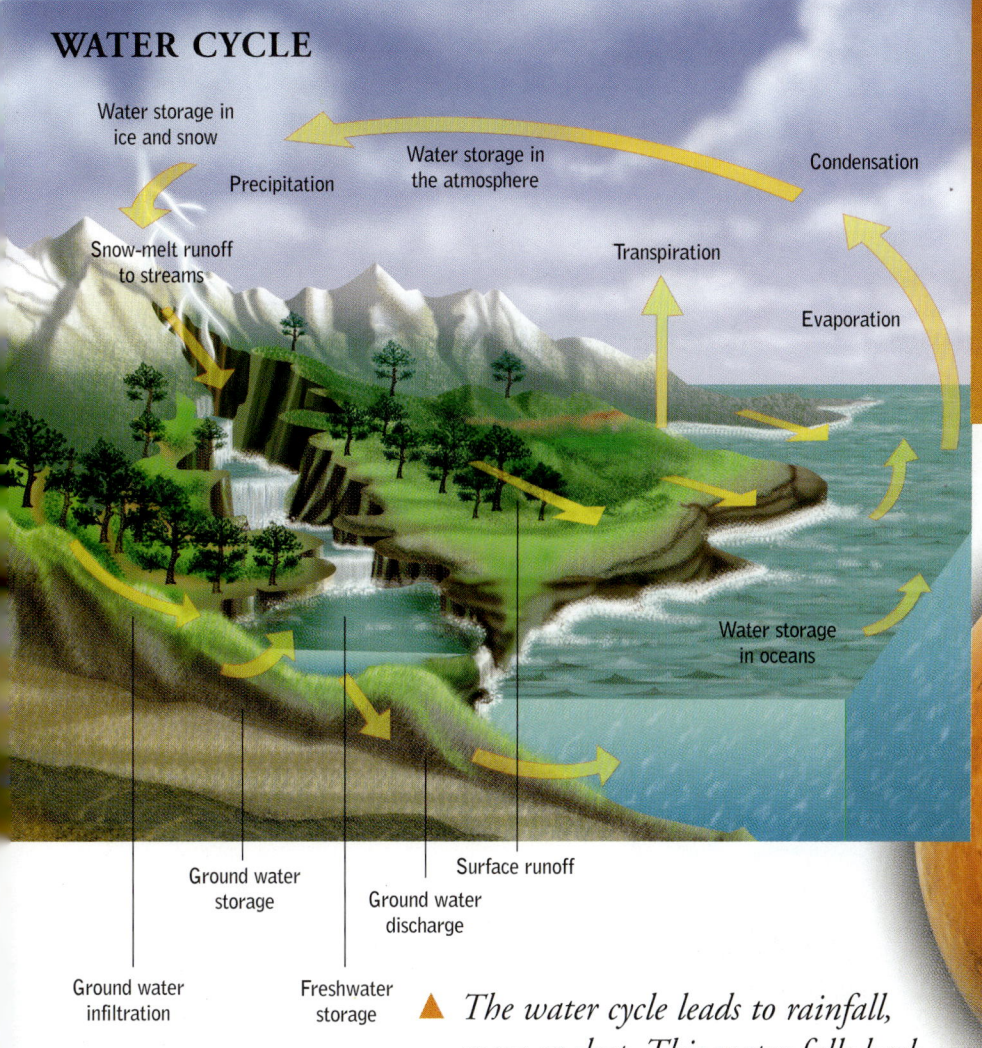

▲ The water cycle leads to rainfall, snow or sleet. This water falls back into rivers, lakes and oceans

Cooling off

As the water vapour rises, the air turns cold and the vapour changes into tiny droplets, forming clouds. When the droplets become too heavy, they fall in the form of rain, hail, sleet or snow. This continuous process makes up the water cycle.

INTERESTING FACT

Like Earth, the planet Mars also has an atmosphere. Research shows a variety of spectacular weather changes on Mars. These include pink skies, ice clouds, giant dust storms and cyclones.

FACT FILE

- On an average, Earth reflects 30 per cent of the Sun's energy back to space
- Fresh snow reflects about 85 per cent of the Sun's energy
- Dry soil reflects about 10 per cent of the Sun's energy
- Clouds reflect upwards of 20 per cent of the Sun's energy

▲ Images from space telescopes show giant dust storms and cyclones on Mars. Wind speed during a dust storm on the planet can be over 200 km/h. Mars has also been found to be cloudy and misty

Wind and Cloud

Wind and cloud are important elements of the weather. When air moves from areas of high pressure to ones of low pressure, it is known as wind. Clouds are formed when rising air cools such that it can no longer hold its water vapour.

Naming by direction

Some winds occur in a particular direction, and are named after the direction they blow from. An easterly wind blows from the east and a westerly wind blows from the west.

Gusty winds

As a basic rule, the greater the pressure difference, the stronger the wind. Wind speeds are measured using an instrument called an anemometer.

▼ *Wind speeds can vary greatly, from gentle evening breezes to tearaway storms. The higher the pressure difference, the more powerful the wind*

◀ Wind speed is measured by an instrument called the anemometer. The three cups on it catch the wind, causing it to rotate. Anemometers should be placed about nine metres (30 feet) above the ground

Clouded in

Clouds are formed when water vapour condenses in the form of tiny droplets. They can be white, light grey or dark in colour, and come in various shapes and sizes. Wispy clouds are called cirrus and heaped ones are known as cumulus. Clouds that appear in layers are stratus clouds. There are 10 types of clouds based on height and shape.

Rain bearer

Not all clouds are rain-bearing. Clouds that have the word 'nimbus', either in the beginning or the end of their names, are rain clouds. Usually, cumulonimbus clouds are the most dangerous. They can cause hail, lightning, tornadoes, downdraughts, downbursts and flash floods.

INTERESTING FACT

In the desert, temperatures can rise to extremes, producing short-lived whirlwinds. Such winds form a spiralling column of hot air and rarely last for more than a few minutes.

FACT FILE

- **Sea breeze** can cause an 8°C to 11°C drop in temperature in 30 minutes
- **Highest wind speed:** 372 km/h, measured at Mt Washington
- **Whirlwind height:** More than 100 metres (330 feet)
- **Windiest place:** Commonwealth Bay, Antarctica Coast. Wind speeds there reach 119 km/h
- **Cirrus clouds** are formed at the highest levels, at 9,144 metres (30,000 feet) or more

TYPES OF CLOUDS

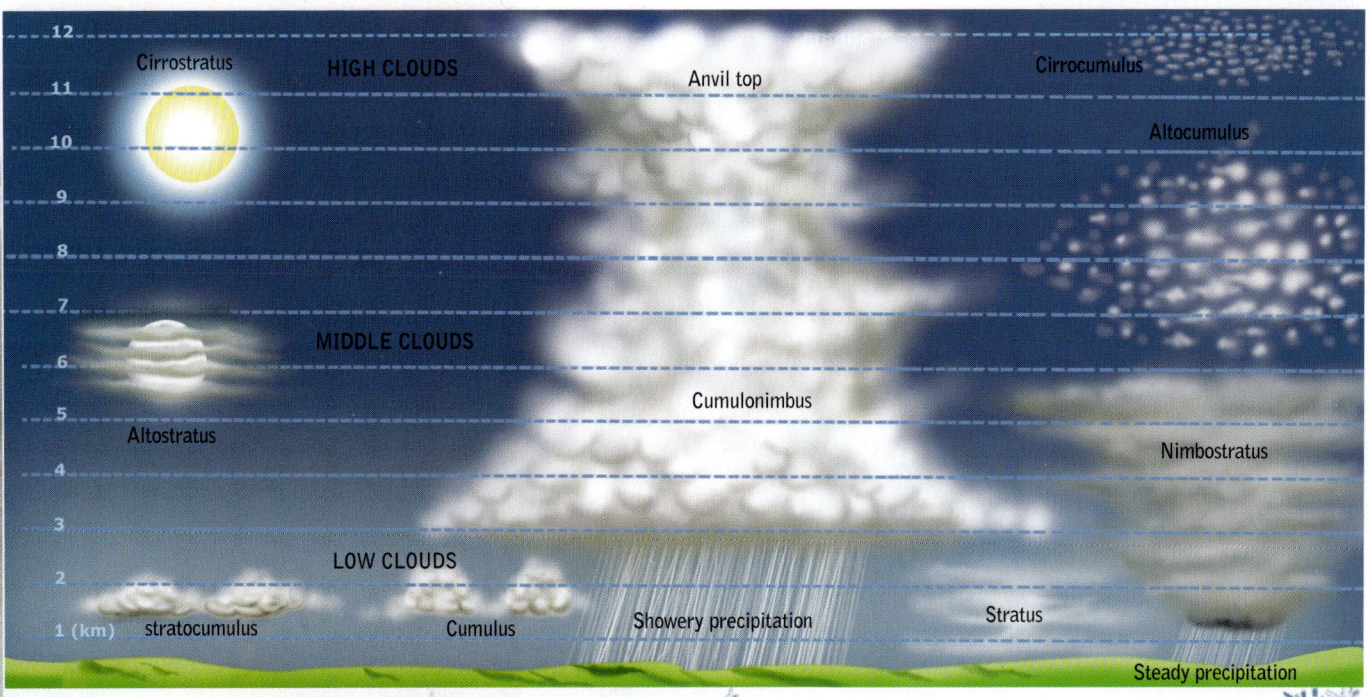

Seasons

Each of the four seasons – spring, summer, autumn and winter – has different weather conditions. Seasons occur due to the Earth's tilted axis as it goes around the Sun. The regions tilted towards the Sun have summer, while those away have winter.

▲ *Due to the Earth's elliptical orbit around the Sun, different parts receive varying amounts of sunlight, and for varying durations. This is how seasons occur*

Hot and cold

In the spring, days are warm in the Northern Hemisphere. Summer follows, with hot days and warm nights. In autumn the days become cooler, gradually leading to a cold winter. When the Northern Hemisphere has winter, the Southern has summer.

▶ *Changing weather conditions indicate the beginning of a new season. As autumn draws to a close, daily temperatures fall steadily to signal the onset of winter*

Four or two

Some regions on Earth do not witness all the four seasons. In the tropics, temperatures change only slightly. But the amount of rainfall varies, and these regions have wet and dry seasons. The polar areas have light and dark seasons. The sun shines almost all the time in summer, and never during winter.

Extreme conditions

Summer is the warmest season of the year, while winter is the coldest. Polar winters are freezing, while summers in desert regions can rise above 50 degree Celsius!

▼ *The polar region gets sunlight only during the summer season. Winters are long, dark and bitterly cold*

AUTUMN

WINTER

INTERESTING FACT

In the early days, people looked at the sky for signs of a new season. The bright star Regulus, which climbs above the eastern horizon, signals the beginning of spring in the Northern Hemisphere. The square of Pegasus indicates that autumn is near, while Aldebaran is a sure sign of winter.

FACT FILE

- **Spring:** Late March–early June (NH); Sept–early Dec (SH)
- **Summer:** Late June–early Sept (NH); late Dec–early March (SH)
- **Autumn:** Late Sept–Nov (NH); March–early June (SH)
- **Winter:** Dec–early March (NH); late June–early Sept (SH)

(NH)=Northern Hemisphere
(SH)=Southern Hemisphere

Blissful weather

Autumn is the season between summer and winter. Autumn days are warm and nights are cool. As winter approaches, frost often occurs at night. Spring is another pleasant season.

▲ *Nature is at its best during spring, with near-perfect weather. Flowers bloom during this season, and hibernating animals wake up from their winter naps*

Climates

> ▼ *Desert climates are marked by extremely hot days and cold nights and, usually, strong winds*

The weather conditions of a certain region over a long period of time are collectively called climate. An area's climate tells us about the kinds of plants and animals that can survive there. The study of climate is called climatology.

Latitudinal point

The Sun plays a crucial role in a region's climate. A region's latitude, or position north or south of the Equator, determines the angle at which the Sun's rays will strike. This creates different climatic conditions.

◄ *People who live in cold, snowy areas often use skis, sleds or snowmobiles for transportation*

Other factors

Regions with the same latitude may have different climates, depending on the presence of a water body. For instance, the inland area of a continent may be warmer in summer than the coast, which is cooled by the ocean air. Mountain areas also have a different climate.

Types of climate

World climates can be divided in many ways. Five broad groups are: tropical, dry, warm temperate, cold temperate and cold. Each of these is often further divided into subgroups.

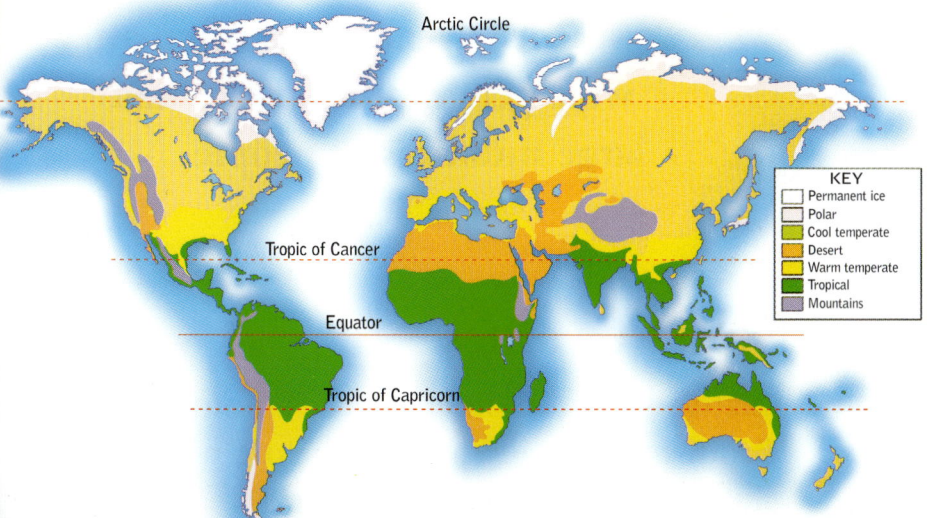

INTERESTING FACT

The Antarctic is the coldest and windiest place in the world. Temperatures there fall well below -50°C. In summer, temperatures stay well below the freezing point.

FACT FILE

- **Climate change** affects sea levels, which are rising by 1.5 mm per year
- **Tropical climates** occur near the Equator
- **Cold climates** occur near the poles, the subarctic region and the mountains
- About 80 per cent of the world's population live in temperate zones

◀ *The houses people live in are also made to suit the area's climate. In rainy places, houses may have a steep, pointed roof so that the rainwater can drain off easily*

Broad classifications

Areas with tropical climates are warm throughout the year, with no winters. Places with cold climates face long and severe winters. Desert areas have dry climates, with little or no rainfall. Warm temperate areas have warm and wet summers and mild winters. Cold temperate climates are characterised by less extreme temperatures and frequent rainfall.

Humid and Hot

Extreme heat can be a life-threatening condition, though it is not as dramatic as other forms of severe weather. Heat waves often affect wide geographical areas and large numbers of people.

Relative values

Relative humidity refers to the amount of moisture the air can hold before it rains. The most it can hold is 100 per cent. Relative humidity in desert areas can be as low as 20 per cent.

◀ *Heat waves can lead to fatal heatstrokes if precautions are not taken*

Humidity factor

The amount of water vapour in the air is called humidity. The more moisture there is in the air, the higher the humidity. The amount of moisture that the air can hold depends on its temperature. Cooler air holds less moisture.

▶ *The best way to tackle heat waves is to stay in the shade and drink lots of water*

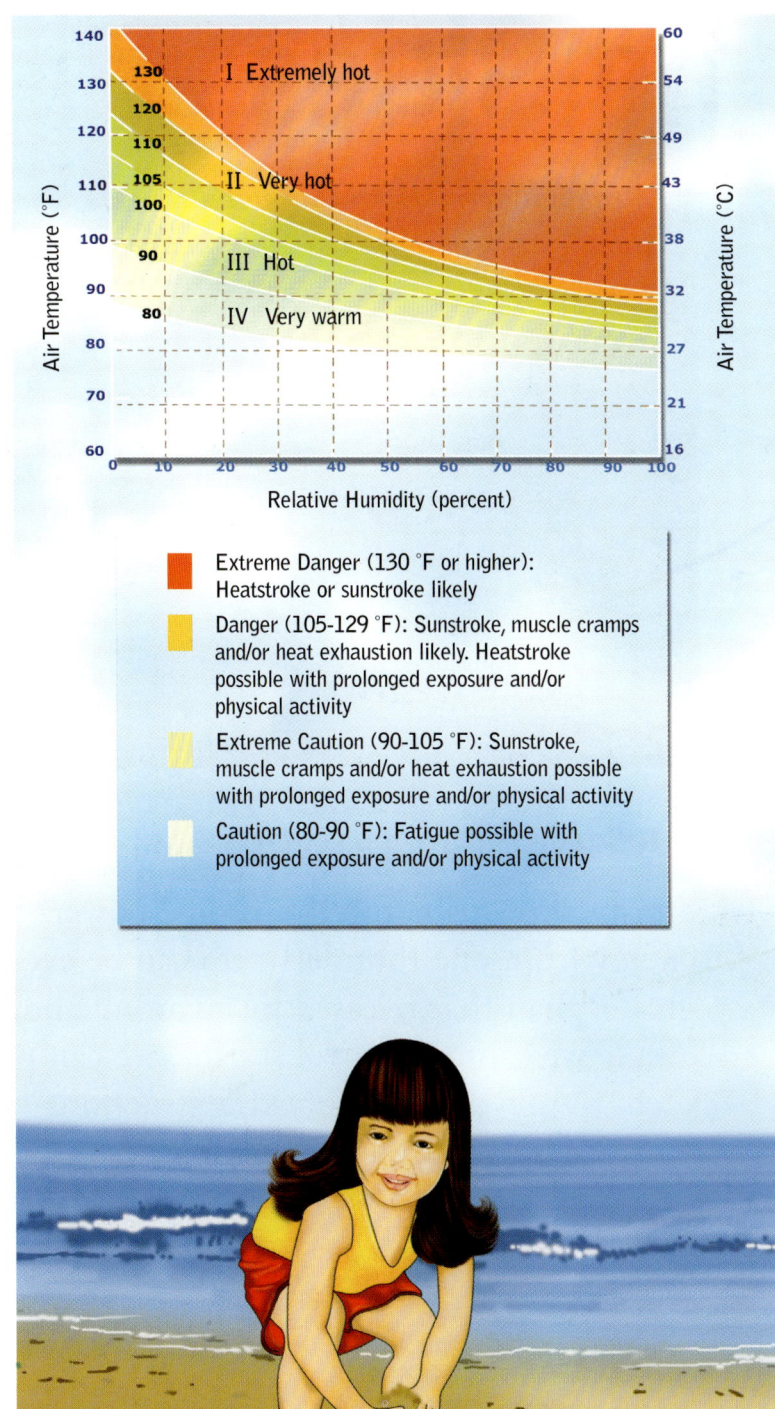

INTERESTING FACT

On calm, clear nights, the air just above the ground cools rapidly. If the temperature of this air falls below the dew point, it settles as dewdrops on grass, leaves, windows and other surfaces.

FACT FILE

- **Caution:** At 29°C to 34°C – physical activity may cause fatigue
- **Extreme Caution:** At 35°C to 41°C – long exposure can cause heat cramps and/or exhaustion
- **Danger:** Above 41°C – can lead to possible heat stroke with long exposure; heat exhaustion and heat cramps likely

Dewy point

The temperature at which the air becomes saturated is called the dew point. If the temperature falls below the dew point, the moisture in the air condenses.

Heat index

The heat index combines temperature and relative humidity to give an idea of what it would feel like under normal-to-low humidity conditions. High and dangerous heat indices occur mostly during summer.

Storming the Skies

Storms are one of the most fascinating and dangerous of all weather conditions. Thunderstorms can uproot trees, while cyclones can destroy entire towns. Storms reflect weather at its wildest!

▼ *A tropical storm occurs in tropical regions. It has gusty winds, strong enough to uproot trees*

Long and short of it

Storms vary in size and duration. The smallest ones – tornadoes and thunderstorms – usually affect areas of about 25 square kilometres and last for a few hours. The largest storms – hurricanes or cyclones – may affect whole continents and last for weeks.

Devastating power

Storms show us nature's awesome power. The energy from one thunderstorm can be even greater than that released by an atomic bomb! While we cannot control storms, we can predict them to prevent widespread destruction.

▶ *Most tornadoes in the Northern Hemisphere spin counter-clockwise, while in the Southern Hemisphere they are clockwise*

Turning tornadoes

The tornado in the *Wizard of Oz* carried Dorothy to a new land. While tornadoes in real life can hardly do that, they can be quite devastating. In a tornado, the wind column forms a narrow funnel that spins like a top and is in contact with the ground.

▲ *The best way to protect oneself during a tornado is to take cover in the basement at home, or even under the stairway*

INTERESTING FACT

Hurricanes are called typhoons in the Western Pacific; baquios in the Philippines; willy-willies in Australia; and cyclones in India. The word 'hurricane' itself comes from a West Indian name.

FACT FILE

- **Tornado** speeds can go up to 300 mph (483 km/h)
- **Hurricane** speeds are over 74 mph (119 km/h)
- **Tropical storms** occur at 39 mph (63 km/h)
- **Speed of gales** is between 28 and 55 knots (50-102 km)

Hurried hurricane

Hurricanes are violent, spiralling storms that are set off when warm air rises over the sea to form huge clouds. More air rushes below the rising air and starts to spiral at high speeds. When these fierce winds hit the land, they destroy everything in their path.

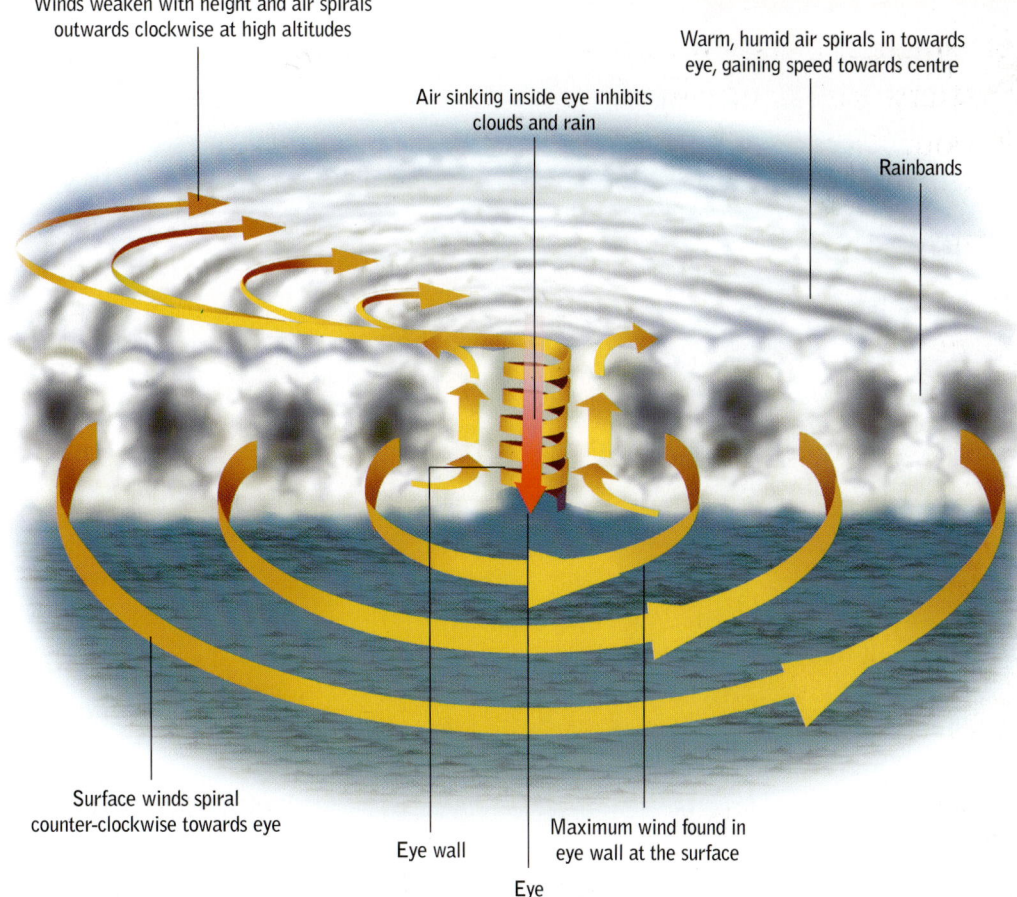

▲ *A hurricane can extend across hundreds of miles. Hurricanes have a clear centre, called the eye, where air sinks in*

Thunder and Lightning

Thunderstorms are violent, short-lived weather disturbances. They occur when layers of warm, moist air rise in a large, swift updraft to cooler regions of the atmosphere.

Downdraft of wind

As it rises, the moisture condenses to form towering clouds. When the droplets become very heavy, a downpour follows. Columns of cooled air then sink earthward, striking the ground with strong winds or a thunderstorm.

▶ Lightning can strike tall trees and burn them up

▶ Not all lightning hits the ground. Cloud-to-ground lightning makes up about 10 per cent of all lightning. Other types include cloud-to-cloud and those that occur within the cloud

Lightning flash

Thunderstorms are accompanied by lightning. It is caused when ice crystals in the clouds rub together, creating electricity and causing a flash of lightning. This then heats up air, causing a loud rumble called thunder.

- Long metallic rods are often placed on the roofs of tall buildings to prevent lightning from striking them. The rods intercept the flashes and guide the current to the ground through cables

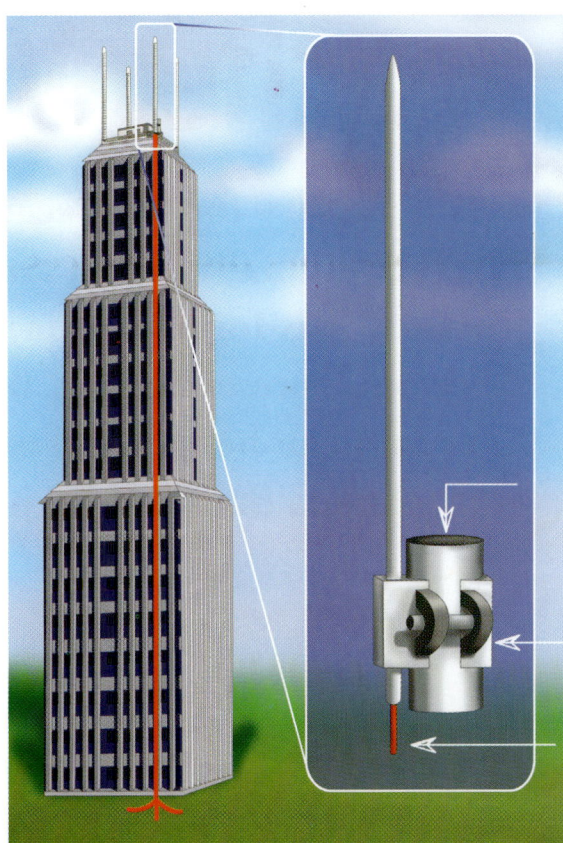

INTERESTING FACT

You see lightning long before hearing the thunder because light travels faster than sound. To check how far away a storm is, count the seconds between lightning and the sound of thunder. Divide the number of seconds by five to know the distance in miles, or by three for kilometres.

FACT FILE

- As many as 1,800 **thunderstorms** occur in the world at any given point of time
- **Lightning** can strike targets 16 or even 40 km away from its parent cloud
- **Thunderstorms** can produce 100 strokes of lightning every second
- **Longest lightning bolt:** 190 km, measured in Dallas, U.S.
- **Thunderstorm speeds:** 19 km/h to 161 km/h

Rare sights

Some rarely seen types of lightning include red sprites and blue jets. However, you cannot see either of them with the naked eye.

- If you are stuck in the open during a lightning, do the lightning crouch. Put your heels together and squat down. Then tuck your head and cover your ears. When the threat of lightning passes, get to a safe spot

Striking force

Lightning strikes tall things, like trees and buildings. So if you are caught in a thunderstorm, crouch on the ground to avoid being hit. But never take shelter under a tree.

Weather Wash

Rain is necessary for life because it provides water for human beings, animals and plants. It is formed from the water vapour present in air. But too much rain can be harmful as well, causing floods that destroy property and life.

◀ *The shape of a raindrop depends on its size. Raindrops with a diameter of less than 1 millimetre are round. Larger raindrops become flatter as they fall*

Drops keep falling

Raindrops vary greatly in size as also in the speed with which they fall. The larger the raindrop is, the faster it falls. Raindrop size varies between 0.50-6.40 millimetres in diameter.

Monsoon showers

Seasonal rainfall, especially in regions near the tropics, is caused by special winds called monsoons. The monsoon that blows across Southern Asia in the summer brings extremely heavy rainfall.

◀ *Raincoats help you stay dry even in heavy rainfall*

Flooded away

A flash flood is caused by sudden, excessive rainfall that sends a river, stream or any other water body out of its banks. Often, this occurs in a short period of time. This can be deadly, particularly when floods arrive without warning.

INTERESTING FACT

Weather conditions, combined with a spring tide, produced one of the worst floods on the east coast of England in 1953. Over 300 people lost their lives in this disaster. The flooding was caused by a storm surge.

FACT FILE

- **Highest rainfall in a minute:** 3.1 cm, at Unionville, U.S.
- **Highest rainfall in a day:** 182.5 cm, in Foc-Foc, la Reunion, in the Indian Ocean
- **Highest rainfall in a month:** 930 cm, in Cherrapunji, India
- **Highest rainfall in a year:** 2,647 cm, in Cherrapunji, India
- **Lowest rainfall in a year:** 0.03 inches, in Arica, Chile

Keeping a tab

Weather forecasters play a very important role in the reduction of flood losses. By issuing storm and flood warnings, they aim to minimise destruction and the loss of life.

◄ *Boats, rafts and helicopters are used to rescue people marooned by the rising waters in a flood*

As Cold as Can Be

Teeth-chattering and bone-chilling temperatures are yet another extreme in the changing moods of weather. During the Ice Age, the entire Earth was covered with snow. While that period ended about 15,000 years ago, some parts of the Earth like Greenland, Siberia and Antarctica still have snow through the year.

Ice covering

The snow on the ground is constantly rearranged by wind, temperature and the weight of snow itself. If the snow grows denser, after surviving spring and summer melting for years, it turns into ice to form glaciers.

Sliding avalanches

Even solid ice and layers of snow can be dangerous, just like avalanches are. An avalanche is a moving mass of snow that may contain ice, soil, rocks and uprooted trees.

Smashing snow

An avalanche is set off when an unstable mass of snow breaks away from a mountainside and moves downhill. The growing river of snow picks up speed as it rushes down the mountain.

◀ *The height of a mountain, the steepness of its slope, and the type of snow on it determine the likelihood of an avalanche*

SNOW-COVERED REGIONS (SHADED IN WHITE) ACROSS THE GLOBE...

▼ *during the Ice Age*

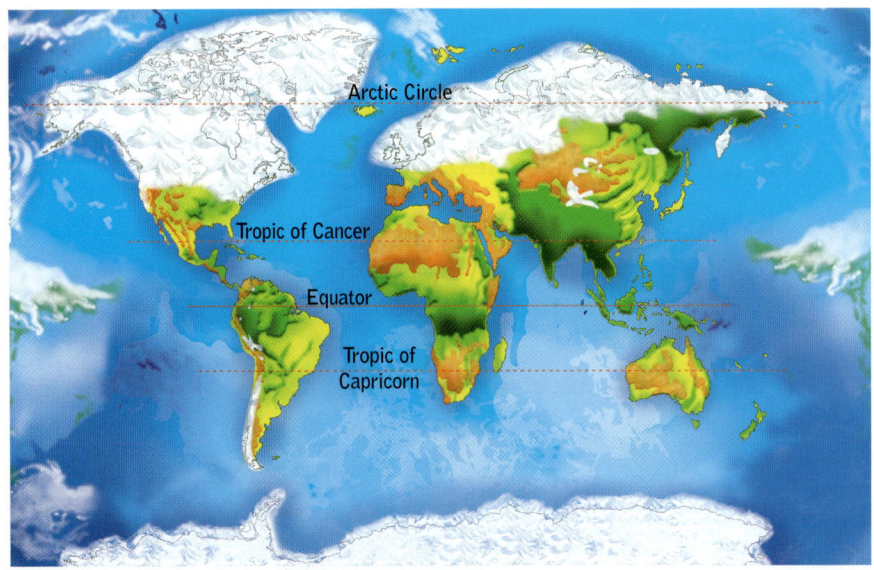

INTERESTING FACT

The climate between the years 1550 and 1750 in England was known as the Little Ice Age, when the winters were so cold that the Thames froze. This allowed for Frost Fairs on the frozen river, complete with tents, sideshows and food stalls. The last such fair was held in the winter of 1813-14.

FACT FILE

- About 90 per cent of the world's **ice** is found in Antarctica
- **Snow** covers about 23 per cent of the Earth's surface
- **Frost** occurs at temperatures below freezing point
- **Avalanche speeds:** Up to 245 mph (394 km/h)

Protective role

Snow protects crops such as winter wheat from hard frosts and cold, dry winds. People in Greenland and northern Canada live in igloos, or houses built from snow.

▼ *at present*

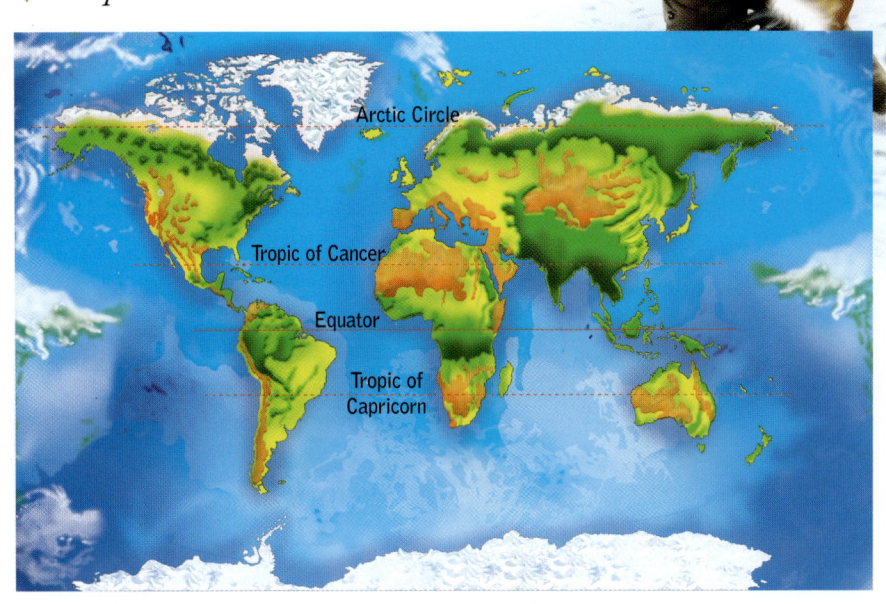

▲ *It is a lot of fun to play with snow. You can build snowmen or have snow fights!*

25

Snow, Hail and Ice

While rain is the most common form of precipitation, different weather conditions cause the water to fall in different states – be it snow, hail, or even ice. While snow and ice fall only when temperatures touch freezing points, hail can fall in summers too.

White as snow

If the temperature of clouds is below freezing, ice crystals are formed. These crystals can turn to snow if the temperature of air near the ground is about 2.8°C. If the temperature is in the region of 2.8°C-3.9°C, the crystals change to sleet or ice pellets.

Intricate snowflakes

Snowflakes are collections of as many as a hundred ice crystals. The heaviest snowfalls occur when the temperature is around the freezing point.

▲ *All snowflakes have six sides, but no two are the same and each forms an intricate design*

INTERESTING FACT

Blizzards are snowstorms with high winds and low temperatures. The wind may also pile the snow into huge drifts, thereby blocking roads.

FACT FILE

- Large **hailstones** can fall at rates of up to 90 mph (145 km/h)
- **Largest known hailstone:** 2¼ pounds
- Severe **blizzards** have temperatures of -12°C (10° F) or lower
- You would need to melt 20 to 40 inches of **dry snow** to equal one inch of rain

◀ *Blowing snow in blizzards makes it impossible to see more than a short distance. Blizzards can have windspeeds of over 72 km/h (45 mph), with near-zero visibility*

Ice storms

Winter storms include ice storms and blizzards. Most ice storms occur when the temperature is just below freezing. In such a storm, precipitation falls as rain, but freezes as it hits the ground. This creates a coating of ice on the ground and streets, making them slippery and often causing traffic accidents.

Hailstorms

Yet another form of precipitation is hail. Hail forms when strong air currents carry ice crystals up and down between the top and bottom layers of a thundercloud. The crystals become larger and larger, until they fall to the Earth as hailstones.

When Storms Strike

Over the years, hurricanes and tornadoes have played havoc with millions of lives. Here's a look at some of the most devastating storms to have hit mankind.

Big storm

The biggest storm to hit England occurred in November 1703. The winds are believed to have exceeded 193 km/h (120 mph), leaving behind a trail of devastation. As many as 8,000-15,000 people are believed to have been killed in the storm.

▼ *During Hurricane Galveston, the weather bureau office gauge also blew away after recording wind speeds of 160 km/h (100 mph). It was a night that completely destroyed Texas City*

America's worst

The worst weather disaster in America was the Category 4 hurricane that hit Galveston, Texas, on September 8, 1900. More than 8,000 people died when a 15-foot storm surge flooded the island.

◀ Since hurricanes cause a lot of damage, scientists try to predict them with the help of many devices. A Scatterometer is one such instrument that is placed on a satellite. It sends out radar beams to Earth and measures the ones that are reflected back. This in turn is used to measure wind speeds and direction

INTERESTING FACT

Meteorologists usually give hurricanes special names. These names are reused unless the storm is particularly destructive. They used to be mainly women's names, but since 1979, hurricanes have also been given men's names.

FACT FILE

Hurricane categories
- **Category One:** Winds 119-153 km/h (80-95 mph)
- **Category Two:** Winds 154-177 km/h (96-110 mph)
- **Category Three:** Winds 178-209 km/h (111-130 mph)
- **Category Four:** Winds 210-249 km/h (131-155 mph)
- **Category Five:** Winds greater than 249 km/h (155 mph)

Hurricane Hugo

Hurricane Hugo slammed into South Carolina, U.S., in 1989. The storm had begun off the coast of Africa and travelled across the Caribbean. Wind speeds as high as 257 km/h (160 mph) were recorded. The damages cost the state about $5 billion.

Super Outbreak

The 1974 Super Outbreak spawned 148 tornadoes, the largest number ever produced by a single storm system in the United States. Thirty of these tornadoes were classified as F4 or F5 on the Fujita-Pearson Scale. Before the rampage was over, more than 300 lives were lost in 13 US states and Canada.

Drought Disasters

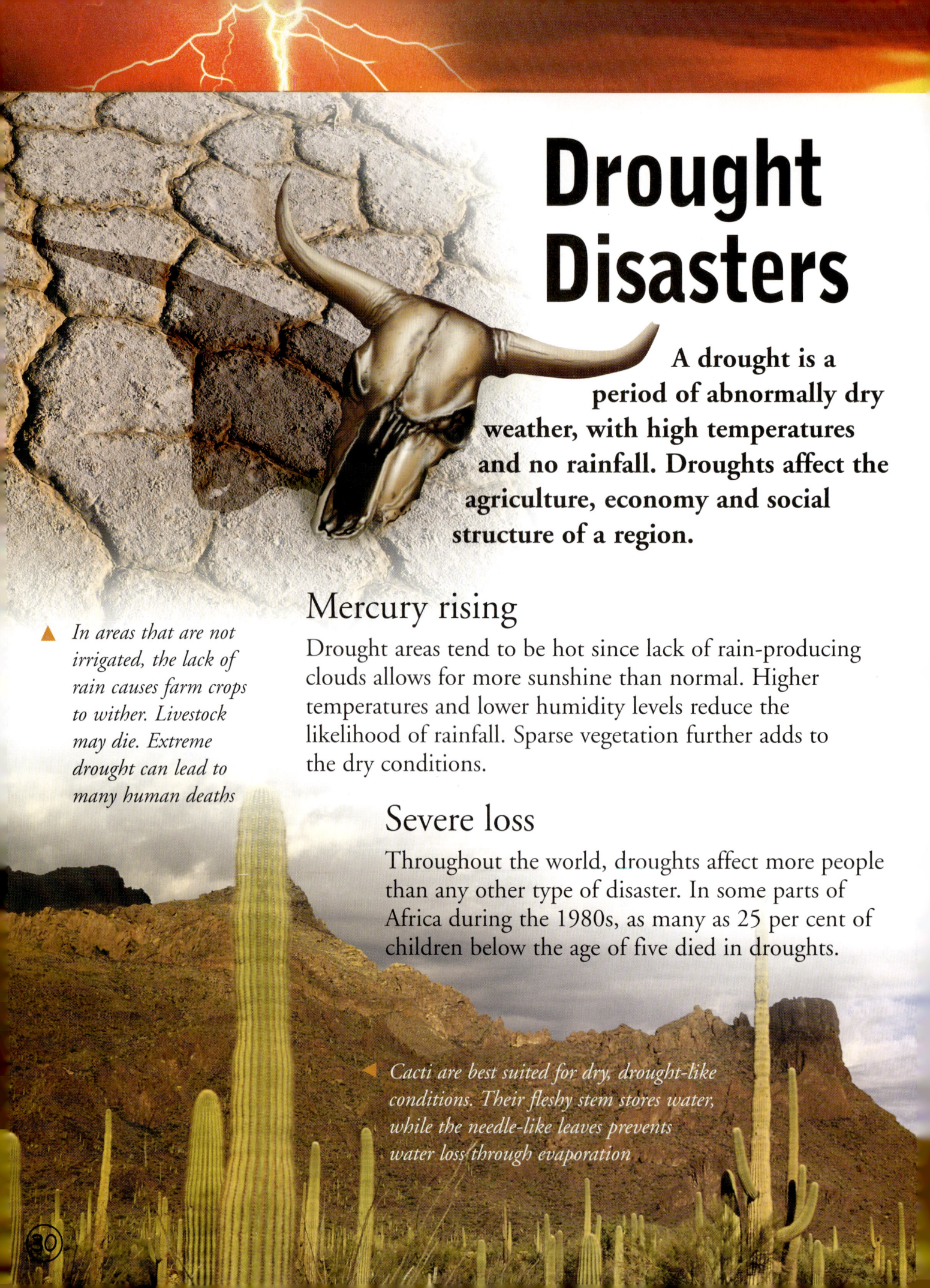

A drought is a period of abnormally dry weather, with high temperatures and no rainfall. Droughts affect the agriculture, economy and social structure of a region.

In areas that are not irrigated, the lack of rain causes farm crops to wither. Livestock may die. Extreme drought can lead to many human deaths

Mercury rising

Drought areas tend to be hot since lack of rain-producing clouds allows for more sunshine than normal. Higher temperatures and lower humidity levels reduce the likelihood of rainfall. Sparse vegetation further adds to the dry conditions.

Severe loss

Throughout the world, droughts affect more people than any other type of disaster. In some parts of Africa during the 1980s, as many as 25 per cent of children below the age of five died in droughts.

Cacti are best suited for dry, drought-like conditions. Their fleshy stem stores water, while the needle-like leaves prevents water loss through evaporation

▲ *To survive severe drought conditions, turtles and frogs dig into the wet mud of a drying river bed or lagoon. Even crocodiles dig into the mud to survive the effects of drought*

High pressure factor

Areas of sinking air create a condition of high pressure that, in turn, leads to dry spells. If the condition continues for a long period, it is termed as a 'blocking high' and can cause droughts. One such case was the drought of 1976 in England, when the total rainfall in London was just 235 millimetres. Temperatures then soared above 32°C.

Tackling drought

Creation of artificial lakes have been suggested to beat droughts. Water evaporating from such lakes might set up a rainfall cycle. Another method that has been tried is cloud seeding, an artificial method of bringing about precipitation/rainfall.

INTERESTING FACT

In cloud seeding, iodine crystals are scattered among the clouds from an aircraft. The water vapour molecules in the clouds cluster around the crystals and become heavy, causing the overloaded crystals to fall to the Earth as rain. But it works well only in areas where rainfall occurs naturally.

FACT FILE

SEVERE DROUGHTS
- **Nile drought in Egypt,** 1200-02, over 110,000 people died
- **Potato famine in Ireland,** 1845-49, killed about 1.5 million people
- **Northern China,** 1959-61, about 30 million people died
- **Biafra, Africa,** famine in 1967-69, killed over one million people

▲ *Besides aircraft, cloud seeding has been done from rockets, cannons and ground generators*

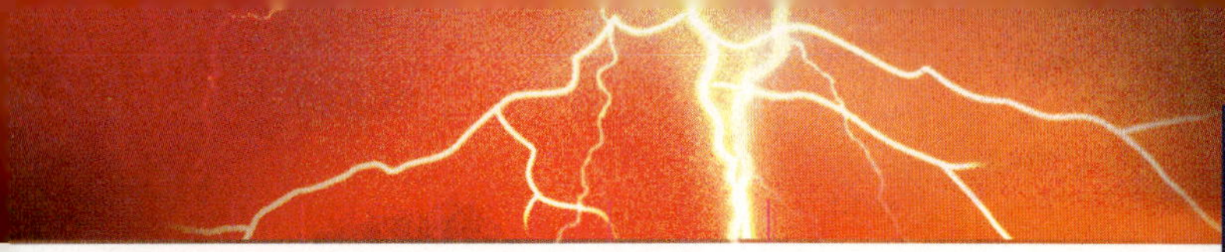

Weather Watch

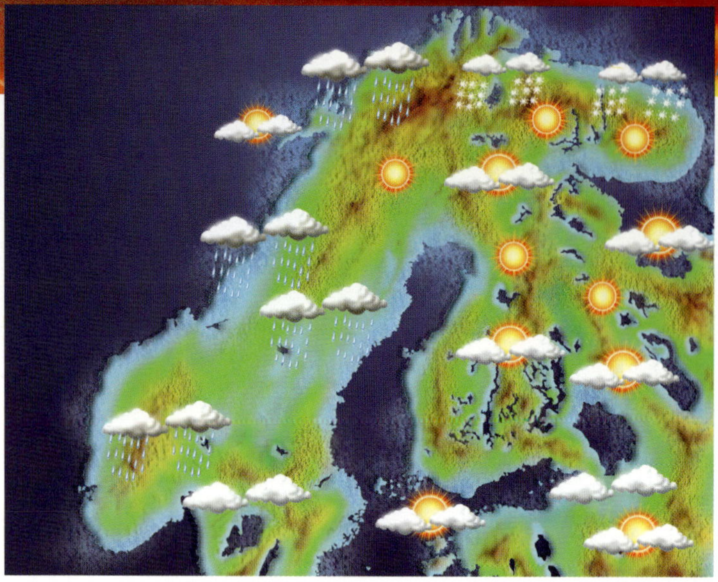

People try to predict weather to prepare in advance for all its extremities. Over 4,000 years ago, people made forecasts based on the position of the stars. Since then, several instruments and technologies have been developed for more accurate predictions.

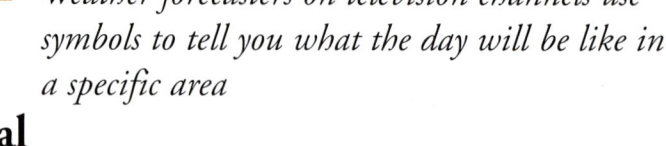

▲ *Weather forecasters on television channels use symbols to tell you what the day will be like in a specific area*

Observation stations

More than 3,500 observation stations record weather conditions on land, using various instruments. Thermometers measure temperature; barometers measure pressure; and anemometers measure wind speed. Weather vanes indicate the direction of winds, while hygrometers measure humidity and rain gauges calculate the amount of rainfall.

Picking up signs

Some observation stations use radar to pick up signs of approaching rains and storms. Satellites also encircle the Earth to convey cloud and temperature patterns. All the data collected is used to create weather maps.

◄ *Every day, observation stations launch two balloons. The balloons are filled with helium, or hydrogen, and measure temperature, air pressure and humidity*

Time factor

In the early 1800s, weather forecasting could not be used to warn people of impending storms. Reports were sent by mail, but the storms usually arrived before the post!

◀ *Painted wooden boxes provide shelter for weather instruments that need to record the temperature and humidity outdoors, but that also need to be kept away from the rain and excessive heat or cold*

INTERESTING FACT

The World Meteorological Organization (WMO), an agency of the United Nations (UN), sponsors the World Weather Watch programme. Through it, weather information is collected by more than 140 nations.

FACT FILE

INSTRUMENTS FOR PREDICTION
- **Rain gauge** was invented before 300 BC
- **Weather vane** was developed by 50 BC
- Galileo developed the **thermometer** in AD 1593
- Edmond Halley made the first **weather map** in 1686
- The first successful **computer forecast** was announced in 1950

Telegraphed reports

The outdated information system received a boost with the telegraph, which enabled meteorologists to send weather observations quickly. In 1856, France became the first country to start a weather service that relied on telegraphed reports. Great Britain began a similar service in 1860.

◀ *Sir Francis Beaufort, an admiral at sea, devised the Beaufort Wind Scale in 1805 to measure the speed of wind. The scale is a series of numbers from 1-13, categorising winds from 'calm' to 'hurricane'*

Eye in the Sky

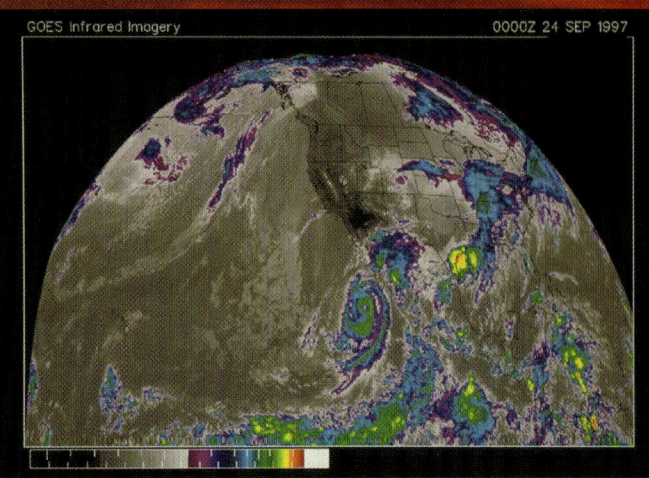

▲ *Images from radars are very effective tools for predicting rain. Weather forecasters study the patterns on radar images to provide warnings on severe thunderstorms, tropical cyclones and areas of heavy rainfall*

Meteorologists use special computers for weather forecasting. These computers function swiftly to receive information from weather stations and satellites. They help to build model weather maps and produce a weather forecast.

In space

Weather stations rely on inputs from artificial satellites placed in orbit about the Earth. Satellites carry television cameras that take pictures of the Earth. These pictures display the pattern of clouds above the Earth as well as large areas of snow and ice on the ground. The photographs allow meteorologists to spot hurricanes and other storms.

Polar-orbiting

There are two main kinds of weather satellites – polar-orbiting and geostationary. Polar-orbiting weather satellites circle the Earth at altitudes between 800 and 1,400 kilometres. They cover up to 10 million square kilometres, or about 2 per cent of the Earth's surface.

▸ *Satellites photograph the surface of the Earth from the skies and these are called satellite images. They show the pattern of winds, clouds and temperatures over the Earth. Meteorologists study these images to predict weather*

▼ Weather planes carry a host of instruments on board. They fly over a region and collect data on temperature, pressure and humidity. They can also drop special sensors that collect data from inside a storm

INTERESTING FACT

There are two main types of forecasts – short-range forecasts and extended forecasts. Short-range forecasts predict the weather over the next 18-36 hours, and are updated several times a day. Extended forecasts cover the next 5, 10 or 30 days, but are not entirely accurate.

FACT FILE

- The **radar** was first used for weather observation in the 1940s
- First weather satellite with a television camera: Tiros I, 1960
- First full-time weather satellite in geostationary orbit: 1974

Weather planes

Other weather observation facilities include aeroplanes and ships. Special weather planes take measurements of atmospheric conditions.

▼ A weather station gets data from satellites, weather planes, observation centres and other sources. Meteorologists keep a track of all these.

In sync

Geostationary satellites, also called geosynchronous satellites, orbit the equator at an altitude of about 35,890 kilometres. At this altitude they can take pictures that cover a much wider area. Pictures from four well-placed geo-stationary satellites can cover the entire Earth at once.

Changing Weather

Weather conditions across the world have evolved over billions of years – from the Ice Age to today's day and age. The earliest changes were a result of natural causes, but in the last century, human beings have played a crucial role in changing weather patterns.

Ice Age

Nearly 50,000 years ago, the Earth was in the middle of its last Ice Age. Much of the Earth's surface was covered in thick sheets of ice, though the temperatures were not bitterly cold. In fact, the snow cover was constant due to cool summers and mild winters.

Interglacial period

The Ice Age ended about 15,000 years ago, when the climate warmed up and the ice melted. We now live in an age called the Interglacial Period. But the next Ice Age is round the corner – just about 1,000 years away!

▶ *Woolly mammoths roamed the Earth during the Ice Age. But as the period ended and the Earth got warmer, it became too hot for the mammoths and they died out about 30,000 years ago*

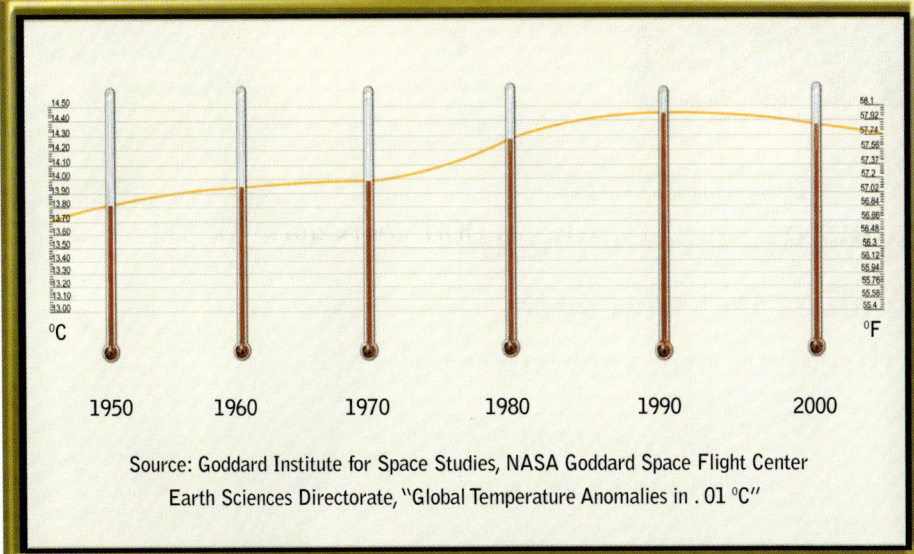

▲ The average temperature of the Earth has been rising over the years. This is because of global warming

▼ Global warming is caused by human actions. High pollution levels from cars and factories cover the surface of the Earth and make it warmer

Slow change

Changes in climate take place gradually through the years. For example, the climate of several areas in North America was somewhat colder in the 1960s and early 1970s, as compared to the 1930s and 1940s.

INTERESTING FACT

Climatic change can be caused by a change in the amount of energy given off by the Sun. Other causes of climatic change include the greenhouse effect and volcanic dust.

FACT FILE

- Total number of **very cold days in the UK** has fallen from 15-20 to around 10 per year
- Average global **sea levels** have increased by 0.1-0.2 metres in the last 100 years
- **Snow cover** in the Northern Hemisphere has decreased by 10 per cent since the 1960s
- By 2100, global **average temperatures** may rise by 1.4°C-5.8°C

Man's role

The changes in Earth's weather pattern, until recently, were a result of nature. However, in recent times, climate conditions have been negatively affected by various human activities.

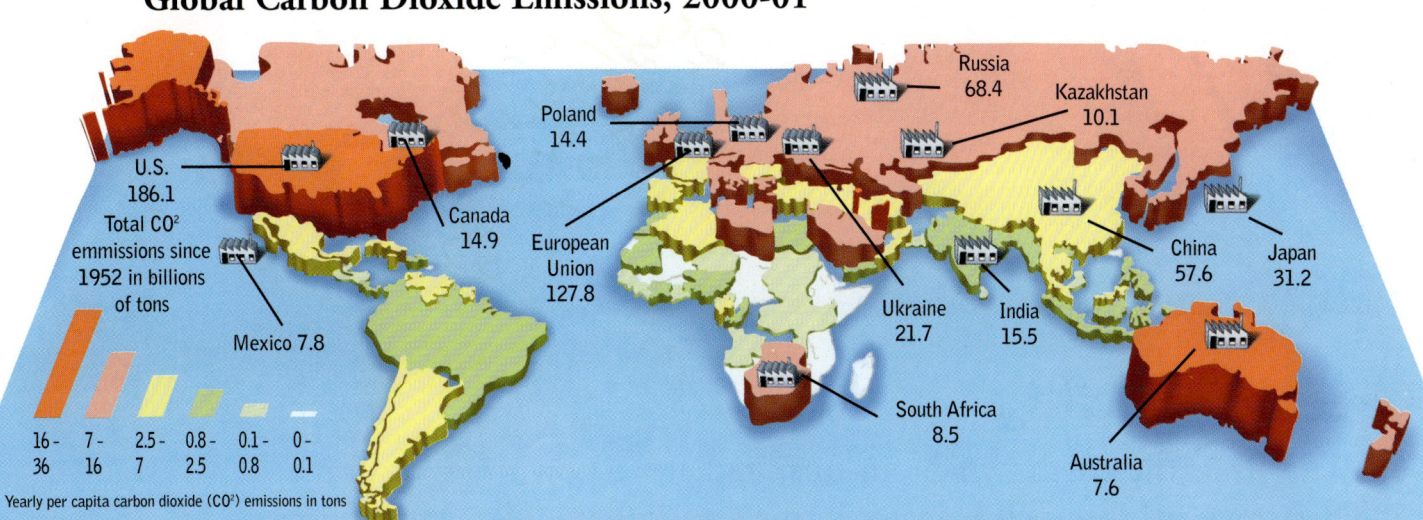

Global Carbon Dioxide Emissions, 2000-01

37

Weather Woes

Changes in weather in recent times, and those predicted over the next 80 years, are largely due to human activity. Environmentalists feel that such changes are likely to pose a threat to our very survival.

Global warming

Far too many greenhouse gases are being produced by industrial activity. These gases are absorbing more heat and warming the Earth far more than is normal, thus leading to global warming. Widespread deforestation (clearing of trees) is also adding to the problem.

▼ *The greenhouse effect is caused by the trapping of heat rays reflected by the Earth. These rays remain in the lower levels of the atmosphere, leading to a state of increased global warming*

Greenhouse effect

The Sun heats the Earth, which, in turn, radiates its own rays of heat. These rays are absorbed by gases in the atmosphere. Like a greenhouse, these gases trap heat and gradually make the climate warmer.

Catastrophes in store

Global warming poses a grave danger to all life forms. Rising temperatures are likely to melt glaciers and cause more rains. This, in turn, would cause a rise in the sea level and, subsequently, floods.

◀ *The burning of fossil fuels like coal and petrol produces carbon dioxide and oxides of nitrogen and sulphur*

INTERESTING FACT

In many places, smoke from factories and vehicle exhausts combine with natural fog to form smog. London, Los Angeles, Tokyo and Mexico City are among the cities that have faced serious smog problems over the years.

FACT FILE

- **Global temperatures** have risen by over 0.7°C in the last 300 years
- Four out of five of the **warmest years** ever recorded were in the 1990s
- **1998** was the warmest year globally
- **1999** was the warmest year recorded in the United Kingdom

Acid rain

Besides rising temperatures, increasing air pollution has also given birth to acid rains. The oxides of sulphur, nitrogen and carbon mix with the moisture in the air to form acids, which are brought down to earth as acid rain. Such rains are extremely harmful to all forms of life.

▲ *The world's forests are being stripped of trees at the rate of 24 square km per hour. This is worsening the greenhouse effect, and may lead to major changes in temperature and rainfall patterns*

Weather or What!

The world has often witnessed a range of bizarre weather phenomena, like snowfall in summer, coloured rain, objects falling from the sky, and much more.

Raining frogs and peaches

While it may never have literally rained cats and dogs, other bodies have been known to shower down. In August 1814, during a storm near Amiens in France, tiny but live frogs came raining down! A similar case was sighted in 1953, in Massachusetts, U.S. In 1961, Louisiana locals claimed to have witnessed an equally strange downpour – of peaches.

Snowy greens

Various parts of the world have reportedly received snowfall in red, green, yellow and brown colours! These colours were said to be caused by tiny vegetable organisms known as Protococcus Nivalis.

▶ Apart from frogs, other creatures that have fallen from the skies include flounders, minnows, snails, mussels, maggots, crayfish, geese and even live snakes!

Colour washout

There have been quite a few instances of coloured rainfall. During a heavy storm in the Shetland Isles, in March 1935, the rain looked like blue-black ink diluted in water! The explanation offered for this was that of pollution. England too witnessed a red-wash on February 21-23, 1903 – caused by dust that blew in from the Sahara.

INTERESTING FACT

It was a case of summer chills in England in 1975, when snow prevented a summer cricket match. At the other extreme, in September 1981, the Kalahari Desert in Africa witnessed snowfall for the first time.

FACT FILE

Falling from the skies
- Green slime reportedly fell out of the sky in Washington, in 1978
- Trowbridge in England received tiny-frog showers on June 16, 1939
- In 1965, a 50-pound mass of ice fell on the Phillips Petroleum Plant in Utah, U.S.
- In 1894, Bath in England received a downpour of jellyfish

El Niño

El Niño refers to the abnormal warming of surface ocean waters in the eastern tropical Pacific. It is believed that El Niño may have led to the 1993 Mississippi floods, the 1998 California floods, and drought conditions in South America, Africa and Australia. Scientists are yet to fully understand the reasons behind the formation of El Niño.

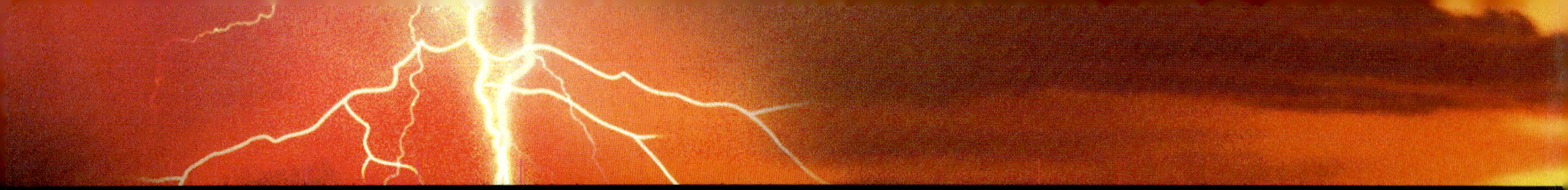

Fascinating Facts

Weather forecasting is not foolproof, since Mother Nature never falls short of surprises. Along with sudden changes in weather conditions, extreme and unusual phenomena make the weather quite unpredictable.

Heat bursts

Heat bursts are phenomena that at times occur during thunderstorms and make conditions hotter. On September 9, 1994, Glasgow in Scotland recorded a temperature of 19º C at 5:02 am. But a heat burst from a nearby storm shot the mercury up to 34º C by 5:17 am.

Spouting water

Another curious occurrence is that of waterspouts. These tornadoes form at sea and are a funnel-like column of air that sucks up sea water and other things in their path. In the past, seamen often mistook waterspouts for monsters rising up from under the ocean!

▶ *People who closely observe a storm brave risky conditions such as high wind, hail, lightning and flying debris*

Rained out

The most rain ever recorded in the United Kingdom in one day was on July 18, 1955. It rained as much as 279 millimetres at Martinstown in Dorset. Of course, this is hardly a patch on the world record of 1,825 millimetres, which fell at Foc-Foc, in la Reunion in the Indian Ocean!

Guiding light

Weather changes at sea can leave ships stranded. Heavy fog or storm-like situations can make even the most experienced mariners lose their way. As a measure to prevent such events from happening, seas and oceans have lighthouses.

INTERESTING FACT

Storm chasers are people who try to get close to storms for purposes of observation. Storm-chasing is dangerous work, but most chasers are very passionate about the phenomena and are willing to embrace the risks.

FACT FILE

- **Highest barometric pressure:** 1083.6 millibars (32inches); Agata, Siberia
- **Odds of being struck by lightning:** About 1 in 800,000
- **Longest-travelling tornado:** 472 km (293 miles), travelled from Missouri to Indiana, U.S.
- Three out of four of all **tornadoes** hit the United States

◀ *Lighthouses are towers that beam lights or sound horns to guide ships to safety while at sea. They are particularly vital during bad weather*

During a storm, there is a simple way to calculate how many miles away the lightning is. Keep a count of the number of seconds between the strike of lightning and the rumbling of thunder, and divide that number by five to get the answer! ▲

Glossary

Altitude: The measure of the height of an object above mean sea level or above the Earth's surface

Antarctica: Area around the geographic South Pole

Arctic: Area around the geographic North Pole

Atmosphere: The air that surrounds the Earth. It chiefly consists of nitrogen and oxygen, and small amounts of other gases, water vapour and dust particles

Autumn: Period between the summer and winter seasons

Blizzard: A blinding snow storm with strong, cold wind

Cirrus: Cirrus clouds typically have a fibrous or hair-like appearance, and often are semi-transparent

Climate: The average weather condition over a long time, usually 10-30 years

Condensation: The process by which water vapour changes from gas to liquid. It is the opposite process to evaporation

Cumulus: Detached clouds, generally dense and with sharp outlines; showing vertical development in the form of domes, mounds, or towers

Dew point: The temperature at which the air becomes saturated. If the temperature falls below the dew point, the moisture in the air condenses

Drifting snow: An uneven distribution of snowfall or existing snow caused by strong surface wind; may occur during or after a snowfall

Drought: A period of abnormally dry weather, with high temperatures and no rainfall

Dust: Small particles of earth or other matter suspended in the air

Equator: The zero-degree latitude on the Earth's surface. It is equidistant from the North and South Poles, and divides the Northern Hemisphere and the Southern Hemisphere

Evaporation: The change in state from liquid to gas

Eye: The calm centre of a hurricane

Fog: A cloud with its base on the Earth's surface. It reduces visibility. If visibility is less than a quarter of a mile, it is termed as dense fog

Forecast: Statement that tries to tell about future occurrences. Weather forecast is based on inputs from various scientific devices

Frost: A thin covering of ice on exposed surfaces when the air temperature really cools down

Geostationary satellite: An orbiting satellite that maintains the same position over the Equator during the Earth's rotation

Gust: A sudden significant increase in, or rapid fluctuation of, wind speed; can vary from 10 knots (11.5 mph) to 16 knots (18 mph) in less than 20 seconds

Heat wave: A period of abnormally hot weather; can last from several days to several weeks

Humidity: Amount of water vapour in the air

Hygrometer: An instrument that measures the water vapour content of the atmosphere

Lightning: A sudden and visible discharge of electricity produced in response to the build-up of electrical potential between cloud and ground; between clouds; within a single cloud; or between a cloud and surrounding air

Meteorologist: Scientist who studies weather conditions

Moisture: Amount of water vapour contained in the air

Monsoon: A southwest wind that brings heavy rains

Pressure: The force per unit area exerted by the weight of the atmosphere above a point on or above the Earth's surface

Radar: Acronym for Radio Detection And Ranging. A system for detecting the direction, range or presence of objects, by sending out pulses of high-frequency electromagnetic waves. These waves are reflected back by the object

Rain gauge: An instrument used to measure the amount of rain that has fallen. Measurement is done in hundredths of inches (0.01")

Satellite: Any object that orbits a celestial body. The term is often used in reference to manufactured objects that orbit the Earth

Sleet: Occurs when ice pellets fall along with rain or snow; 5 millimetres or less in diameter

Troposphere: Lowest level of the atmosphere; extends from the surface of the Earth up to 10-16 kilometres

Weather: The condition of air surrounding a particular area over a short period; can span a few hours to a few days